WEAPONS OF WAR

WEAPONS OF
WORLD
WAR I

BY MATT DOEDEN

CAPSTONE PRESS
a capstone imprint

Blazers Books are published by Capstone Press,
1710 Roe Crest Drive, North Mankato, Minnesota 56003
www.mycapstone.com

Library of Congress Cataloging-in-Publication Data
Names: Doeden, Matt, author.
Title: Weapons of the World War I/ by Matt Doeden.
Description: North Mankato, Minnesota: Capstone Press, [2017] | Series: Blazers. Weapons of
    War | Includes bibliographical references and index.
Identifiers: ISBN 978-1-5157-7907-0 (library hardcover) | ISBN 978-1-5157-7918-6 (eBook PDF)
Subjects: LCSH: Military weapons—History—20th century—Juvenile literature.
    World War, 1914–1918—Equipment and supplies—Juvenile literature.
Classification: U815 .D64 2018
LC record available at https://lccn.loc.gov/2016055798

Editorial Credits
Bradley Cole, editor; Kyle Grenz, designer; Jo Miller, media researcher;
Gene Bentdahl, production specialist

Photo Credits
Alamy: Chronicle, 21 (bottom right), Classic Stock, 9; Corbis via Getty Images: Corbis/Hulton
Deutsch Collection, 15; Dreamstime: Mccool, 20 (bottom right); DVIC: Lt. Adrian C. Duff (Army),
23, NARA, 12, 25 (bottom), 29 (top right); Getty Images: Hulton Archive, 10, Imagno, 28, Photo 12,
16 (bottom), Popperfoto, 29 (bottom right); iStockphoto: duncan1890, 26, richjam, cover (bottom
left); Newscom: akg-images, 18, Glasshouse Images, 16 (top), Heritage Images/The Print Collector,
6, 21 (top), NHilary Jane Morgan, 27, picture alliance/Archiv/Berliner Verlag, 24; Shutterstock:
CreativeHQ, 13 (middle left), Darq, 21 (middle right), Everett Historical, 5, 20 (bottom left and top), 25
(top), 29 (top left), frescomovie, cover (bottom right), Gary Blakeley, cover (left), Jeffrey B. Banke, 11
(bottom), KWJPHOTOART, cover (top), Militarist, 11 (top), 13 (middle and top), Olemac, 13 (bottom),
Peter Lorimer, cover (right), Zerbor, cover (middle), Zsolt Horvath, 13 (middle right); SuperStock:
Underwood Archives, 21 (bottom left); The Image Works/Topham, 29 (middle right); Wikimedia: Bain
News Service/LOC, 29 (bottom left)

Design Elements: Shutterstock: autsawin uttisin, Bennyartist, Dinga, donatas1205, joephotostudio,
mamanamsal, Milan M, Paladin12, Sergey Andrianov

Printed and bound in China
PO004598

TABLE OF CONTENTS

Battle in the Trenches . . . 4

Infantry Weapons 8

Infantry Weapons and Gear . . . 13

Battlefield Blasts 14

Heavy Weapons
and Explosives 20

From Land to Sea
and Sky 22

Vehicles 29

Glossary 30
Read More 31
Internet Sites 31
Index 32

Battle in the Trenches

The clatter of gunfire fills the air on a World War I (WWI) battlefield. Soldiers duck down in **trenches**. They all hope to live through the day.

trench—a long, deep area cut into the ground with dirt piled up on one side; WWI armies dug trenches for a place to take cover

WWI trenches in Serbia

4

FACT

World War I was also called "The Great War" and "The War to End all Wars."

FACT

France, Great Britain, Russia, and the United States were key players in WWI. These Allied nations fought the Central Powers, which included Germany, Austria-Hungary, and Turkey.

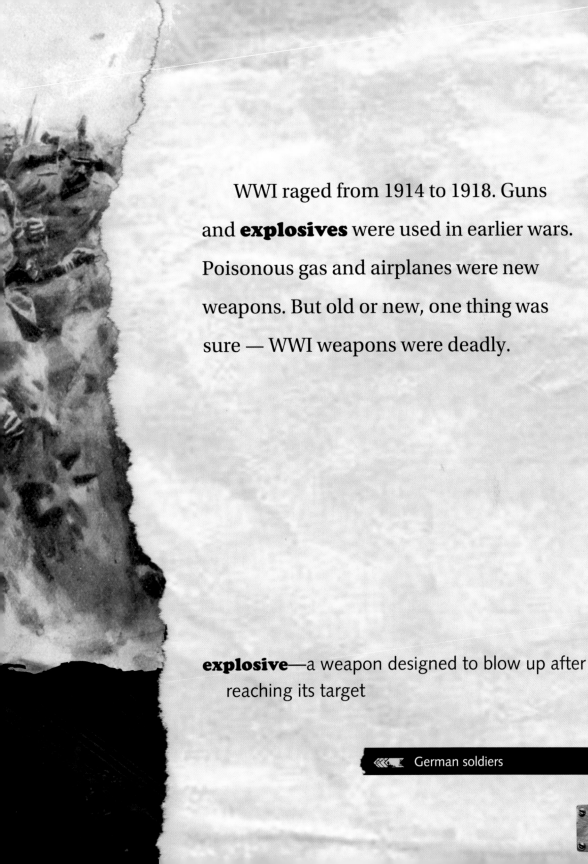

WWI raged from 1914 to 1918. Guns and **explosives** were used in earlier wars. Poisonous gas and airplanes were new weapons. But old or new, one thing was sure — WWI weapons were deadly.

explosive—a weapon designed to blow up after reaching its target

German soldiers

Infantry Weapons

A WWI **infantry** soldier was never without his **rifle**. Soldiers used these guns to hit distant targets. U.S. soldiers pitted their Springfield M1903 rifles against the Germans' Mauser rifles.

infantry—the part of an army that fights on foot

rifle—a powerful gun with a long barrel that is fired from the shoulder

a soldier with his rifle and bayonet ⟫⟫⟫

FACT

Armies used poisonous gas for the first time in WWI. Soldiers wore gas masks to protect themselves.

Soldiers used other guns to shoot at closer targets. Pistols like the German Luger and the U.S. M1911 were easy to handle. British soldiers used their Webley Model 1887 at close range.

GERMAN LUGER »

« BRITISH WEBLEY 1887

German flamethrowers struck fear into soldiers everywhere. These long tubes spouted burning fuel. Hand grenades were another threat. Soldiers tossed or fired these small explosives into enemy trenches.

FACT

Flamethrowers shot fire almost 50 feet (15 meters).

INFANTRY WEAPONS AND GEAR

⌃ **RUSSIAN MOSIN-NAGANT RIFLE**

≪ **U.S. HAND GRENADE**

GAS MASK ≫

≪ **GERMAN HAND GRENADE**

⌃ **RUSSIAN BAYONET**

 French soldiers using liquid fire from their trench

Battlefield Blasts

Trenches were **filthy**. But staying put kept soldiers safe from machine gun fire. These large guns shot hundreds of bullets each minute.

filthy—very dirty

The rumble of explosives was constant. **Cannons** called **mortars** rained shells onto soldiers. Anti-aircraft guns blasted **missiles** at enemy airplanes.

cannon—a large, heavy gun usually mounted on wheels or another supporting structure

mortar—a short cannon that shoots small, explosive shells

missile—an explosive weapon thrown or launched at a distant target

top image: British soldiers in action
bottom image: German mortar team

When it came to cannons, **howitzers** were king. The German cannon Big Bertha shot shells more than 7 miles (11 kilometers) away. Some of its shells weighed more than 250 pounds (113 kilograms)!

howitzer—a large cannon with a long barrel; howitzers fire shells high into the air and at distances of several miles

German soldiers next to a howitzer

HEAVY WEAPONS AND EXPLOSIVES

⌃ **U.S. ANTI-AIRCRAFT MACHINE GUN**

⌃ **BRITISH HEAVY GUN**

⌃ **RUSSIAN MACHINE GUN**

⌃ RUSSIAN HOWITZER

PRUSSIAN ≫
HOWITZER

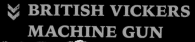
BRITISH VICKERS
MACHINE GUN

⌃ GERMAN KRUPP SIEGE
MORTAR

From Land to Sea and Sky

Tanks were a new weapon. These **armored** vehicles on tracks often broke down. At first, they did little damage. But their big guns helped armies push through enemy lines later in the war.

armored—having a protective covering; WWI tanks had metal armor

American troops going into battle on a Renault FT-17 tank ▶▷▷▷

Other weapons traveled through the air. Airplane pilots shot each other down and dropped bombs. The Germans attacked from airships called zeppelins.

a New Zealand pilot attacking a zeppelin

a German pilot dropping a bomb from his plane

Warships blasted each other with gunfire. Submarines hid silently underwater. They shot **torpedoes** at enemy supply ships.

torpedo—an explosive missile that travels underwater

British battleship HMS *Centurion*

FACT

Submarine crews watched out for sea mines. Bumping one would cause a deadly explosion.

a British submarine

From rifles to airplanes, World War I was filled with deadly weapons. In 1918, the war ended. But updated models of its weapons proved their power in later wars.

FACT

More than 8 million soldiers died during WWI.

VEHICLES

⏷ BRITISH BIPLANE

⏶ U.S. TANK

⏷ GERMAN ZEPPELIN

⏷ BRITISH SUBMARINE

⏶ U.S. BATTLESHIP

Glossary

armored (AR-muhrd)—having a protective covering; WWI tanks had metal armor

cannon (KAN-uhn)—a large, heavy gun usually mounted on wheels or another supporting structure

explosive (ik-SPLOH-siv)—a weapon designed to blow up after reaching its target

filthy (FILTH-ee)—very dirty

howitzer (HOU-uht-sur)—a large cannon with a long barrel; howitzers fire shells high into the air and at distances of several miles

infantry (IN-fuhn-tree)—the part of an army that fights on foot

missile (MISS-uhl)—an explosive weapon that is thrown or launched at a distant target

mortar (MOR-tur)—a short cannon that shoots small, explosive shells

rifle (RYE-fuhl)—a powerful gun with a long barrel that is fired from the shoulder

torpedo (tor-PEE-doh)—an explosive missile that travels underwater

trench (TRENCH)—a long, deep area cut into the ground with dirt piled up on one side; WWI armies dug trenches for a place to take cover

Read More

Adamson, Thomas K. *World War I*. Wars in U.S. History. Mankato, Minn.: Childs World, 2015.

Edwards, Susan Bradford. *Trench Warfare*. Essential Library of World War I. Minneapolis, Minn.: Essential Library, 2016.

Summers, Elizabeth. *Weapons and Vehicles of World War I*. Tools of War. North Mankato, Minn.: Capstone Press, 2016.

Internet Sites

FactHound offers a safe, fun way to find Internet sites related to this book. All of the sites on FactHound have been researched by our staff.

Here's all you do:

Visit *www.facthound.com*

Type in this code: 9781515779070

Check out projects, games and lots more at
www.capstonekids.com

Index

airplanes, 7, 16, 25, 28

airships

   See zeppelins

Allied nations, 7

anti-aircraft guns, 16

barrage balloons, 25

bayonets, 9

bombs, 25

bullets, 14

cannons, 16, 19

   howitzers, 19

   mortars, 16

Central Powers, 7

explosives, 7, 12, 16, 27

flamethrowers, 12

gas masks, 11

hand grenades, 12

infantry, 8

machine guns, 14

missiles, 16

pistols, 10

   Lugers, 10

   M1911s, 10

poisonous gas, 7, 11

rifles, 8, 9, 28

   Mausers, 8

   Springfield M1903s, 8

sea mines, 27

shells, 16, 19

shotguns, 10

tanks, 22, 23

torpedoes, 26

trenches, 4, 12, 14

warships, 26

   submarines, 26

   supply ships, 26

zeppelins, 25